I0539139

There's Poetry in Self-Discovery

A JOURNEY OF REFLECTION AND GROWTH

BY
KRISTINA HARDY

Copyright© 2025 by Kristina E. Hardy.
Print Book ISBN: 979-8-218-62199-5
There's Poetry in Self-Discovery: A Journey of Reflection
and Growth
All rights reserved. This workbook is intended for
personal use only. No part of this publication may be
reproduced, distributed, or transmitted in any form or by
any means, including photocopying, recording, or other
electronic or mechanical methods, without the prior
written permission of the author.

How to use this Workbook

THIS WORKBOOK IS DIVIDED INTO FOUR IDENTICAL SECTIONS TO HELP YOU TRACK YOUR PERSONAL GROWTH AND EVOLVING PERSPECTIVES OVER TIME. COMPLETE THE FIRST SECTION FULLY. THEN PAPERCLIP IT CLOSED.

IN THREE MONTHS, RETURN TO THE NEXT SECTION AND GO THROUGH THE EXERCISES AGAIN— WITHOUT LOOKING BACK AT YOUR PREVIOUS ANSWERS. ONCE YOU'VE FINISHED, COMPARE YOUR RESPONSES TO THE FIRST SECTION. NOTICE WHAT HAS CHANGED, WHAT HAS STAYED THE SAME, AND WHERE YOU FEEL CALLED TO REFLECT MORE DEEPLY.

ONLY YOU HOLD THE ANSWERS YOU SEEK. THIS PROCESS ISN'T ABOUT RIGHT OR WRONG—IT'S ABOUT DISCOVERING WHERE YOU ARE ON YOUR JOURNEY, WHAT MATTERS MOST TO YOU, AND HOW YOU WANT TO GROW. EVERYTHING YOU NEED IS ALREADY WITHIN YOU.

Section One

REMEMBER TO COMPLETE THIS SECTION FULLY BEFORE MOVING ON, AND DON'T FORGET TO PAPERCLIP 📎 WHEN YOU'RE DONE!.

Rising from the Deep

SHE SWAM THROUGH WATERS, DARK AND DEEP,

WHERE SHADOWS CURLED AND SILENCE WEEPED.

YET WITH EACH STROKE, HER SPIRIT GREW,

FOR DARKNESS FORGED WHAT LIGHT ONCE KNEW.

EMERGING, BREATHLESS, ON THE SHORE,

SHE FELT THE WEIGHT OF FEAR NO MORE.

THE NIGHT HAD SHAPED HER, FIERCE AND FREE—

A STRENGTH SHE NEVER THOUGHT COULD BE.

Self Discovery

WHAT FEELING OR IMAGE DOES THIS POEM EVOKE ABOUT YOU?

_____

_____

_____

_____

_____

_____

WHAT STRENGTH OR RESILIENCE DO YOU SEE REFLECTED IN THE POEM?

_____

_____

_____

_____

_____

_____

Self Discovery

———— ❖ — ❖ ————

HOW CAN YOU APPLY THE MESSAGE OF THIS POEM TO YOUR OWN LIFE?

_____

_____

_____

_____

_____

_____

_____

WHAT DOES THE PHRASE "DARKNESS FORGED WHAT LIGHT ONCE KNEW" MEAN TO YOU?

_____

_____

_____

_____

_____

_____

_____

Self Discovery

---◆◆◆—————◆◆◆---

RE-READ THE POEM, AND DRAW THE FIRST THING THAT COMES TO MIND:

(It's not about how well you draw, it's about self reflection. Use words and symbols if it helps. This is about you and your feelings.)

One with the Infinite

SHE GAZED UPON THE ENDLESS SKY.

A SEA OF STARS SO VAST. SO HIGH.

FOR A MOMENT. SHE FELT SO SMALL.

A FLEETING SPARK. A WHISPERED CALL.

BUT THEN THE NIGHT BREATHED SOFT AND TRUE.

ITS QUIET PULSE. A GENTLE CLUE——

SHE WAS NOT ALONE. NOT SET APART.

BUT WOVEN DEEP WITHIN ITS HEART.

THE COSMOS HUMMED. THE HEAVENS SWAYED.

AND IN THEIR DANCE. HER SOUL OBEYED.

NOT LOST. NOT LESS. NOT CAST ASIDE——

BUT PART OF ALL. THE ENDLESS TIDE.

Self Discovery

WHAT FEELING OR IMAGE DOES THIS POEM EVOKE ABOUT YOU?

_____

_____

_____

_____

_____

_____

HOW DOES THIS POEM MAKE YOU FEEL ABOUT YOUR PLACE IN THE UNIVERSE?

_____

_____

_____

_____

_____

_____

Self Discovery

WHAT DOES THE LINE "PART OF ALL, THE ENDLESS TIDE" MEAN TO YOU?

_____

_____

_____

_____

_____

_____

HOW DOES FEELING LONELY DIFFER FROM BEING ALONE, AND HOW DOES THIS AFFECT YOU?

_____

_____

_____

_____

_____

_____

Self Discovery

RE-READ THE POEM, AND DRAW YOURSELF IN THE UNIVERSE::

(It's not about how well you draw, it's about self reflection. Use words and symbols if it helps. This is about you and your feelings.)

The Beauty in Difference

WE STAND AS SISTERS. SIDE BY SIDE.

THE SAME IN HEART. IN LOVE. IN PRIDE.

YET IN OUR THREADS OF GOLD AND LIGHT.

NO TWO ARE WOVEN QUITE ALIKE.

YOUR FIRE BURNS. MY RIVER FLOWS.

YOUR PETALS BLOOM. MY WILD WIND BLOWS.

AND IN THE SPACES WHERE WE PART.

LIES THE BRILLIANCE OF OUR ART.

NOT MEANT TO BLEND. NOR FADE AWAY.

BUT SHINE IN OUR OWN FEARLESS WAY.

FOR EVERY VOICE. FOR EVERY HUE.

THE WORLD IS BRIGHTER——WITH ME AND YOU.

Self Discovery

---◆◆◆---

WRITE WHAT THIS POEM MEANS TO YOU, AND APPLY IT TO ONE ASPECT OF YOUR LIFE:

_____

_____

_____

_____

_____

_____

_____

WHAT 'FIRE BURNS' OR 'RIVER FLOWS' WITHIN YOU? WHAT MAKES YOUR SPIRIT UNIQUELY VIBRANT?

_____

_____

_____

_____

_____

_____

Self Discovery

WHAT DOES THE LINE "AND IN THE SPACES WHERE WE PART, LIES THE BRILLIANCE OF OUR ART." MEAN TO YOU?

_____

_____

_____

_____

_____

_____

DO YOU FEEL LIKE FITTING IN MEANS TO EMULATE OTHERS OR DO YOU TRY TO FIND SOMETHING SIMILAR BUT DIFFERENT WITHIN YOURSELF?

_____

_____

_____

_____

_____

_____

Self Discovery

RE-READ THE POEM, AND WRITE DOWN A STRENGTH IN EACH BOX AND 3-5 THINGS YOU CAN/COULD ACCOMPLISH WITH IT (EVEN IF YOU HAVEN'T YET)::

(It's not about how well you draw, it's about self reflection. Use words and symbols if it helps. This is about you and your feelings.)

Dare to Begin

She stands before the towering climb.

A dream so vast. A test of time.

Doubt lingers close. A voice so slight —

What if I'm wrong? What if I'm right?

But mountains rise through wind and stone.

And seeds break earth to stand alone.

No journey starts with certain ground.

But with the courage to be found.

So let her stumble. Let her bend.

Each fall a step. Not journey's end.

For in the cracks. The light shines through —

Proof she is strong. And growing too.

She takes a breath. She dares to try —

For even wings must fail to fly.

Self Discovery

WHAT 'TOWERING CLIMB' OR DREAM IS CALLING TO YOU? WHAT IS THE FIRST STEP YOU NEED TO TAKE TO BEGIN?

_____

_____

_____

_____

_____

_____

WHAT 'VOICE OF DOUBT' IS WHISPERING IN YOUR EAR? HOW CAN YOU FIND THE COURAGE TO QUIET IT AND 'DARE TO BEGIN'?

_____

_____

_____

_____

_____

_____

Self Discovery

THINK ABOUT SOMETHING YOU ACCOMPLISHED, WHICH HAD A FAILED ATTEMPT, AND DESCRIBE WHAT YOU CHANGED TO TURN IT AROUND AND SUCCEED:

_____

_____

_____

_____

_____

_____

HOW DOES THE IDEA THAT "EACH FALL A STEP, NOT JOURNEY'S END" RESONATE WITH YOU?

_____

_____

_____

_____

_____

Self Discovery

RE-READ THE POEM. AND WRITE A 4 STEP PLAN ON HOW YOU CAN CONQUER THE MOUNTAIN -WRITE DETAILS FOR EACH STEP INCLUDE ANY FORESEEABLE PITFALLS. YOU NEED TO HAVE AT LEAST ONE POSSIBLE WAY AROUND IT:

(It's not about how well you draw, it's about self reflection. Use words and symbols if it helps. This is about you and your feelings.)

Found Within

SHE SEARCHED THE WORLD, BOTH FAR AND WIDE,

THROUGH FLEETING JOYS AND CHANGING TIDES,

IN EVERY FACE, IN EVERY PLACE,

SHE CHASED A LIGHT SHE COULD NOT SEE AND COULD NOT TRACE.

SHE REACHED BEYOND, HER HEART UNSURE,

FOR SOMETHING DISTANT, SOMETHING PURE,

YET ALL SHE SOUGHT HAD ALWAYS BEEN——

A QUIET FLAME THAT BURNED WITHIN.

NOT IN ANOTHER, NOT IN THE VIEW,

BUT IN HER OWN HEART, STRONG AND TRUE,

HAPPINESS WHISPERED, SOFT YET CLEAR——

YOU WERE NEVER LOST, I WAS ALWAYS HERE.

Self Discovery

THE POEM DESCRIBES SEARCHING 'THE WORLD, BOTH FAR AND WIDE.' WHERE HAVE YOU LOOKED FOR HAPPINESS OR FULFILLMENT IN YOUR LIFE?

_____

_____

_____

_____

_____

_____

WHAT EXTERNAL THINGS DO YOU SOMETIMES RELY ON FOR HAPPINESS OR VALIDATION? IS IT PEOPLE? FOOD? SHOPPING?

_____

_____

_____

_____

_____

_____

_____

Self Discovery

CAN YOU IDENTIFY WITH THE FEELING OF SEARCHING FOR SOMETHING "DISTANT, SOMETHING PURE"? WHAT DO YOU THINK THAT "SOMETHING" REPRESENTS FOR YOU?

_____

_____

_____

_____

_____

_____

NAME A TIME WHEN YOU HAVE FELT THAT "QUIET FLAME" OF HAPPINESS BURN WITHIN. WHAT SPARKED IT?

_____

_____

_____

_____

_____

_____

Self Discovery

RE-READ THE POEM. NOW, IMAGINE YOUR FLAME AND DRAW IT. USE COLORS THAT REPRESENT THE HAPPINESS AND THE GLOW YOU SEE. FEEL FREE TO ADD THINGS WITHIN YOU THAT FEED THE FLAME:

(It's not about how well you draw, it's about self reflection. Use words and symbols if it helps. This is about you and your feelings.)

Words we Weave

She laughed it off, a casual phrase,

A joke she thought would fade like haze,

Yet words take root, they start to bloom,

And what you speak, your soul consumes.

.

A fleeting slight, a thoughtless jest,

Can carve a doubt within the breast,

Her mind won't question if it's true—

It holds each word and shapes anew.

So let her speak with kindness' art,

To lift herself, to heal, to start,

For every thought, each word she sows,

Becomes the path on which she goes.

Self Discovery

WHAT DOES THE LINE "YET WORDS TAKE ROOT, THEY START TO BLOOM, AND WHAT YOU SPEAK, YOUR SOUL CONSUMES" MEAN TO YOU?.

_____

_____

_____

_____

_____

_____

HOW MIGHT BEING MINDFUL OF 'A FLEETING SLIGHT, A THOUGHTLESS JEST,' CHANGE HOW YOU SPEAK TO AND ABOUT YOURSELF?

_____

_____

_____

_____

_____

_____

Self Discovery

HOW DOES THE IDEA THAT "EVERY THOUGHT, EACH WORD SHE SOWS, BECOMES THE PATH ON WHICH SHE GOES" RESONATE WITH YOU?

_____

_____

_____

_____

_____

_____

RE-READ THE POEM—DOES THE MESSAGE SEEM SILLY OR DOESN'T APPLY TO YOU? IT SO, WHY?

_____

_____

_____

_____

_____

_____

Self Discovery

RE-READ THE POEM. COLLECT 4 THINGS YOU HAVE SAID ABOUT OR TO YOURSELF RECENTLY. PUT THOSE IN THE BOXES ON THE LEFT SIDE. ON THE RIGHT SIDE, WRITE WHAT WOULD YOU HAVE SAID TO A CLOSE FRIEND UNDER SIMILAR CIRCUMSTANCES:

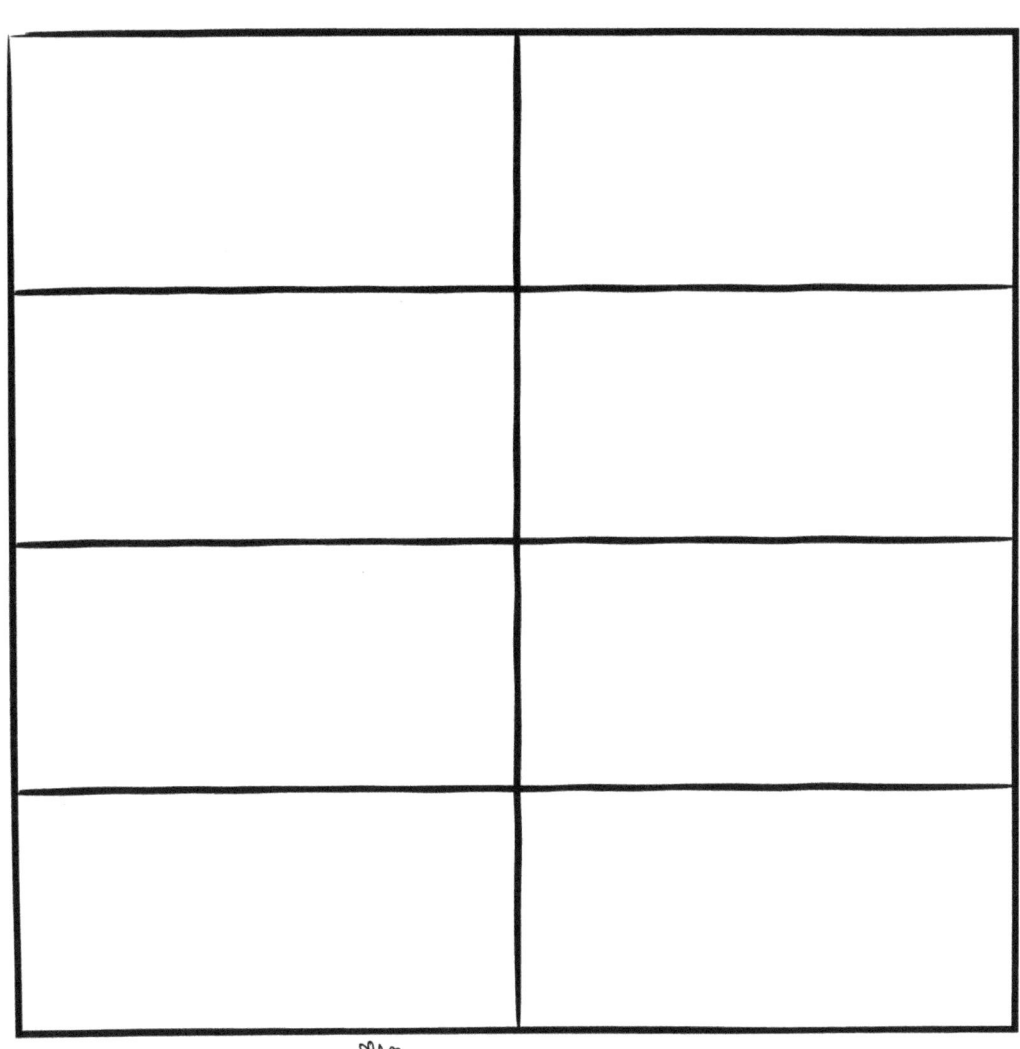

The Gift of Enough

Self-care is more than candle scented air.

More than hands that tame her hair.

It's quiet moments. deep and true.

A gentle grace she's owed. she's due.

It's knowing when her heart is sore.

When less is needed. never more.

It's holding space. it's saying no.

Without the weight of guilt in tow.

To rest. to breathe. to simply be.

Without a goal. a need. a plea.

For she is worthy. whole. and free—

Not just in giving. but in being she.

Self Discovery

THE POEM SUGGESTS SELF-CARE GOES BEYOND PAMPERING. WHAT DOES 'ENOUGH' LOOK LIKE FOR YOU IN TERMS OF CARING FOR YOUR WELL-BEING?

_____

_____

_____

_____

_____

_____

HOW DO SETTING BOUNDARIES AND SAYING 'NO' WITHOUT GUILT CONTRIBUTE TO YOUR OVERALL WELL-BEING AND SENSE OF SELF-WORTH?

_____

_____

_____

_____

_____

_____

Self Discovery

"IT'S HOLDING SPACE. IT'S SAYING NO, WITHOUT THE WEIGHT OF GUILT IN TOW." CAN YOU SET BOUNDARIES AND SAY NO? DESCRIBE THE SCENARIO:

_____

_____

_____

_____

_____

IN THE ABOVE SCENARIO, DID YOU FEEL GUILTY OR FEEL THE NEED TO JUSTIFY OR MAKE IT UP SOMEHOW? EXPLAIN WHY AND WHAT YOU DID TO ALLEVIATE THE FEELING. DO YOU FEEL IT WAS A HEALTHY BALANCE?

_____

_____

_____

_____

_____

Self Discovery

RE-READ THE POEM. IN THE BOXES ON THE LEFT SIDE-LIST 4 EXPRESSIONS OF SELF-CARE YOU WANT TO INCORPORATE IN YOUR LIFE'S ROUTINES. EXPLAIN WHY AND HOW OFTEN YOU WANT TO EXPERIENCE IT. ON THE RIGHT SIDE OF EACH LIST WHAT STEPS OR HOW ARE YOU GOING TO ADD AND MAINTAIN THIS REGIME:

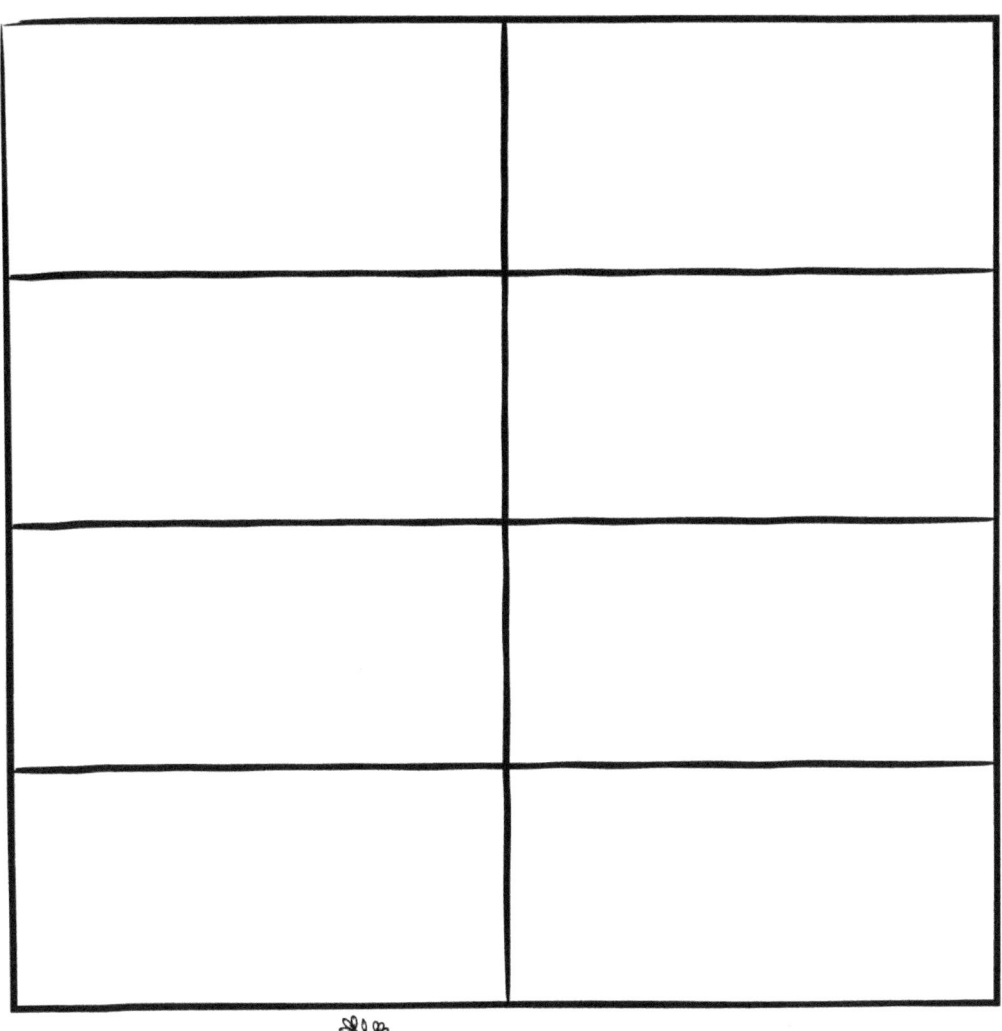

Journal Page

THIS IS YOUR SPACE TO REFLECT. ASK YOUR OWN QUESTIONS.. HERE ARE A FEW TO GET YOUR SELF-EXPLORATION STARTED:

- WHAT SURPRISED ME THE MOST ABOUT MY ANSWERS?

- WHICH POEM OR QUESTION WAS THE HARDEST TO ANSWER AND WHY?

- WHAT RESONATED WITH ME THE MOST?

- WHAT DO I THINK WILL CHANGE THE MOST WHEN I COME BACK FOR THE NEXT SECTION?

REMEMBER THERE IS NO RIGHT OR WRONG ANSWER. THIS IS ABOUT GROWTH AND SELF-REFLECTION

_____

_____

_____

_____

_____

_____

_____

_____

_____

_____

_____

_____

_____

_____

Section Two

REMEMBER TO COMPLETE THIS SECTION FULLY BEFORE MOVING ON. AND DON'T FORGET TO PAPERCLIP  WHEN YOU'RE DONE!.

Rising from the Deep

SHE SWAM THROUGH WATERS, DARK AND DEEP,

WHERE SHADOWS CURLED AND SILENCE WEEPED.

YET WITH EACH STROKE, HER SPIRIT GREW,

FOR DARKNESS FORGED WHAT LIGHT ONCE KNEW.

EMERGING, BREATHLESS, ON THE SHORE,

SHE FELT THE WEIGHT OF FEAR NO MORE.

THE NIGHT HAD SHAPED HER, FIERCE AND FREE——

A STRENGTH SHE NEVER THOUGHT COULD BE.

Self Discovery

WHAT FEELING OR IMAGE DOES THIS POEM EVOKE ABOUT YOU?

_____

_____

_____

_____

_____

_____

_____

WHAT STRENGTH OR RESILIENCE DO YOU SEE REFLECTED IN THE POEM?

_____

_____

_____

_____

_____

_____

_____

Self Discovery

HOW CAN YOU APPLY THE MESSAGE OF THIS POEM TO YOUR OWN LIFE?

_____

_____

_____

_____

_____

_____

WHAT DOES THE PHRASE "DARKNESS FORGED WHAT LIGHT ONCE KNEW" MEAN TO YOU?

_____

_____

_____

_____

_____

Self Discovery

RE-READ THE POEM, AND DRAW THE FIRST THING THAT COMES TO MIND:

(It's not about how well you draw, it's about self reflection. Use words and symbols if it helps. This is about you and your feelings.)

One with the Infinite

SHE GAZED UPON THE ENDLESS SKY.

A SEA OF STARS SO VAST. SO HIGH.

FOR A MOMENT. SHE FELT SO SMALL.

A FLEETING SPARK. A WHISPERED CALL.

BUT THEN THE NIGHT BREATHED SOFT AND TRUE.

ITS QUIET PULSE. A GENTLE CLUE——

SHE WAS NOT ALONE. NOT SET APART.

BUT WOVEN DEEP WITHIN ITS HEART.

THE COSMOS HUMMED. THE HEAVENS SWAYED.

AND IN THEIR DANCE. HER SOUL OBEYED.

NOT LOST. NOT LESS. NOT CAST ASIDE——

BUT PART OF ALL. THE ENDLESS TIDE.

Self Discovery

WHAT FEELING OR IMAGE DOES THIS POEM EVOKE ABOUT YOU?

_____

_____

_____

_____

_____

_____

HOW DOES THIS POEM MAKE YOU FEEL ABOUT YOUR PLACE IN THE UNIVERSE?

_____

_____

_____

_____

_____

_____

Self Discovery

WHAT DOES THE LINE "PART OF ALL, THE ENDLESS TIDE" MEAN TO YOU?

_____

_____

_____

_____

_____

_____

HOW DOES FEELING LONELY DIFFER FROM BEING ALONE, AND HOW DOES THIS AFFECT YOU?

_____

_____

_____

_____

_____

Self Discovery

RE-READ THE POEM, AND DRAW YOURSELF IN THE UNIVERSE::

(It's not about how well you draw, it's about self reflection. Use words and symbols if it helps. This is about you and your feelings.)

The Beauty in Difference

WE STAND AS SISTERS. SIDE BY SIDE.

THE SAME IN HEART. IN LOVE. IN PRIDE.

YET IN OUR THREADS OF GOLD AND LIGHT.

NO TWO ARE WOVEN QUITE ALIKE.

YOUR FIRE BURNS. MY RIVER FLOWS.

YOUR PETALS BLOOM. MY WILD WIND BLOWS.

AND IN THE SPACES WHERE WE PART.

LIES THE BRILLIANCE OF OUR ART.

NOT MEANT TO BLEND. NOR FADE AWAY.

BUT SHINE IN OUR OWN FEARLESS WAY.

FOR EVERY VOICE. FOR EVERY HUE.

THE WORLD IS BRIGHTER——WITH ME AND YOU.

Self Discovery

WRITE WHAT THIS POEM MEANS TO YOU, AND APPLY IT TO ONE ASPECT OF YOUR LIFE:

_____

_____

_____

_____

_____

_____

_____

WHAT 'FIRE BURNS' OR 'RIVER FLOWS' WITHIN YOU? WHAT MAKES YOUR SPIRIT UNIQUELY VIBRANT?

_____

_____

_____

_____

_____

_____

_____

Self Discovery

WHAT DOES THE LINE "AND IN THE SPACES WHERE WE PART, LIES THE BRILLIANCE OF OUR ART," MEAN TO YOU?

_____

_____

_____

_____

_____

_____

DO YOU FEEL LIKE FITTING IN MEANS TO EMULATE OTHERS OR DO YOU TRY TO FIND SOMETHING SIMILAR BUT DIFFERENT WITHIN YOURSELF?

_____

_____

_____

_____

_____

_____

Self Discovery

RE-READ THE POEM, AND WRITE DOWN A STRENGTH IN EACH BOX AND 3-5 THINGS YOU CAN/COULD ACCOMPLISH WITH IT (EVEN IF YOU HAVEN'T YET)::

(It's not about how well you draw, it's about self reflection. Use words and symbols if it helps. This is about you and your feelings.)

Dare to Begin

She stands before the towering climb.

A dream so vast. A test of time.

Doubt lingers close. A voice so slight—

What if I'm wrong? What if I'm right?

But mountains rise through wind and stone.

And seeds break earth to stand alone.

No journey starts with certain ground.

But with the courage to be found.

So let her stumble. Let her bend.

Each fall a step. Not journey's end.

For in the cracks. The light shines through—

Proof she is strong. And growing too.

She takes a breath. She dares to try—

For even wings must fail to fly.

Self Discovery

WHAT 'TOWERING CLIMB' OR DREAM IS CALLING TO YOU? WHAT IS THE FIRST STEP YOU NEED TO TAKE TO BEGIN?

_____

_____

_____

_____

_____

_____

WHAT 'VOICE OF DOUBT' IS WHISPERING IN YOUR EAR? HOW CAN YOU FIND THE COURAGE TO QUIET IT AND 'DARE TO BEGIN'?

_____

_____

_____

_____

_____

_____

Self Discovery

THINK ABOUT SOMETHING YOU ACCOMPLISHED, WHICH HAD A FAILED ATTEMPT, AND DESCRIBE WHAT YOU CHANGED TO TURN IT AROUND AND SUCCEED:

_____

_____

_____

_____

_____

_____

HOW DOES THE IDEA THAT "EACH FALL A STEP, NOT JOURNEY'S END" RESONATE WITH YOU?

_____

_____

_____

_____

_____

Self Discovery

RE-READ THE POEM, AND WRITE A 4 STEP PLAN ON HOW YOU CAN CONQUER THE MOUNTAIN -WRITE DETAILS FOR EACH STEP INCLUDE ANY FORESEEABLE PITFALLS. YOU NEED TO HAVE AT LEAST ONE POSSIBLE WAY AROUND IT:

(It's not about how well you draw, it's about self reflection. Use words and symbols if it helps. This is about you and your feelings.)

Found Within

SHE SEARCHED THE WORLD, BOTH FAR AND WIDE,

THROUGH FLEETING JOYS AND CHANGING TIDES,

IN EVERY FACE, IN EVERY PLACE,

SHE CHASED A LIGHT SHE COULD NOT SEE AND COULD NOT TRACE.

SHE REACHED BEYOND, HER HEART UNSURE,

FOR SOMETHING DISTANT, SOMETHING PURE,

YET ALL SHE SOUGHT HAD ALWAYS BEEN——

A QUIET FLAME THAT BURNED WITHIN.

NOT IN ANOTHER, NOT IN THE VIEW,

BUT IN HER OWN HEART, STRONG AND TRUE,

HAPPINESS WHISPERED, SOFT YET CLEAR——

YOU WERE NEVER LOST, I WAS ALWAYS HERE.

Self Discovery

THE POEM DESCRIBES SEARCHING 'THE WORLD, BOTH FAR AND WIDE.' WHERE HAVE YOU LOOKED FOR HAPPINESS OR FULFILLMENT IN YOUR LIFE?

_____

_____

_____

_____

_____

_____

_____

WHAT EXTERNAL THINGS DO YOU SOMETIMES RELY ON FOR HAPPINESS OR VALIDATION? IS IT PEOPLE? FOOD? SHOPPING?

_____

_____

_____

_____

_____

_____

Self Discovery

CAN YOU IDENTIFY WITH THE FEELING OF SEARCHING FOR SOMETHING "DISTANT, SOMETHING PURE"? WHAT DO YOU THINK THAT "SOMETHING" REPRESENTS FOR YOU?

_____

_____

_____

_____

_____

_____

NAME A TIME WHEN YOU HAVE FELT THAT "QUIET FLAME" OF HAPPINESS BURN WITHIN. WHAT SPARKED IT?

_____

_____

_____

_____

_____

_____

Self Discovery

RE-READ THE POEM. NOW, IMAGINE YOUR FLAME AND DRAW IT. USE COLORS THAT REPRESENT THE HAPPINESS AND THE GLOW YOU SEE. FEEL FREE TO ADD THINGS WITHIN YOU THAT FEED THE FLAME:

(It's not about how well you draw, it's about self reflection. Use words and symbols if it helps. This is about you and your feelings.)

Words we Weave

She laughed it off, a casual phrase,

A joke she thought would fade like haze,

Yet words take root, they start to bloom,

And what you speak, your soul consumes.

.

A fleeting slight, a thoughtless jest,

Can carve a doubt within the breast,

Her mind won't question if it's true—

It holds each word and shapes anew.

So let her speak with kindness' art,

To lift herself, to heal, to start,

For every thought, each word she sows,

Becomes the path on which she goes.

Self Discovery

WHAT DOES THE LINE "YET WORDS TAKE ROOT, THEY START TO BLOOM, AND WHAT YOU SPEAK, YOUR SOUL CONSUMES" MEAN TO YOU?.

_____

_____

_____

_____

_____

_____

HOW MIGHT BEING MINDFUL OF 'A FLEETING SLIGHT, A THOUGHTLESS JEST,' CHANGE HOW YOU SPEAK TO AND ABOUT YOURSELF?

_____

_____

_____

_____

_____

_____

Self Discovery

HOW DOES THE IDEA THAT "EVERY THOUGHT, EACH WORD SHE SOWS, BECOMES THE PATH ON WHICH SHE GOES" RESONATE WITH YOU?

_____

_____

_____

_____

_____

_____

RE-READ THE POEM—DOES THE MESSAGE SEEM SILLY OR DOESN'T APPLY TO YOU? IT SO, WHY?

_____

_____

_____

_____

_____

Self Discovery

———— ◦●◦ ◦●◦ ————

RE-READ THE POEM. COLLECT 4 THINGS YOU HAVE SAID ABOUT OR TO YOURSELF RECENTLY. PUT THOSE IN THE BOXES ON THE LEFT SIDE. ON THE RIGHT SIDE. WRITE WHAT WOULD YOU HAVE SAID TO A CLOSE FRIEND UNDER SIMILAR CIRCUMSTANCES:

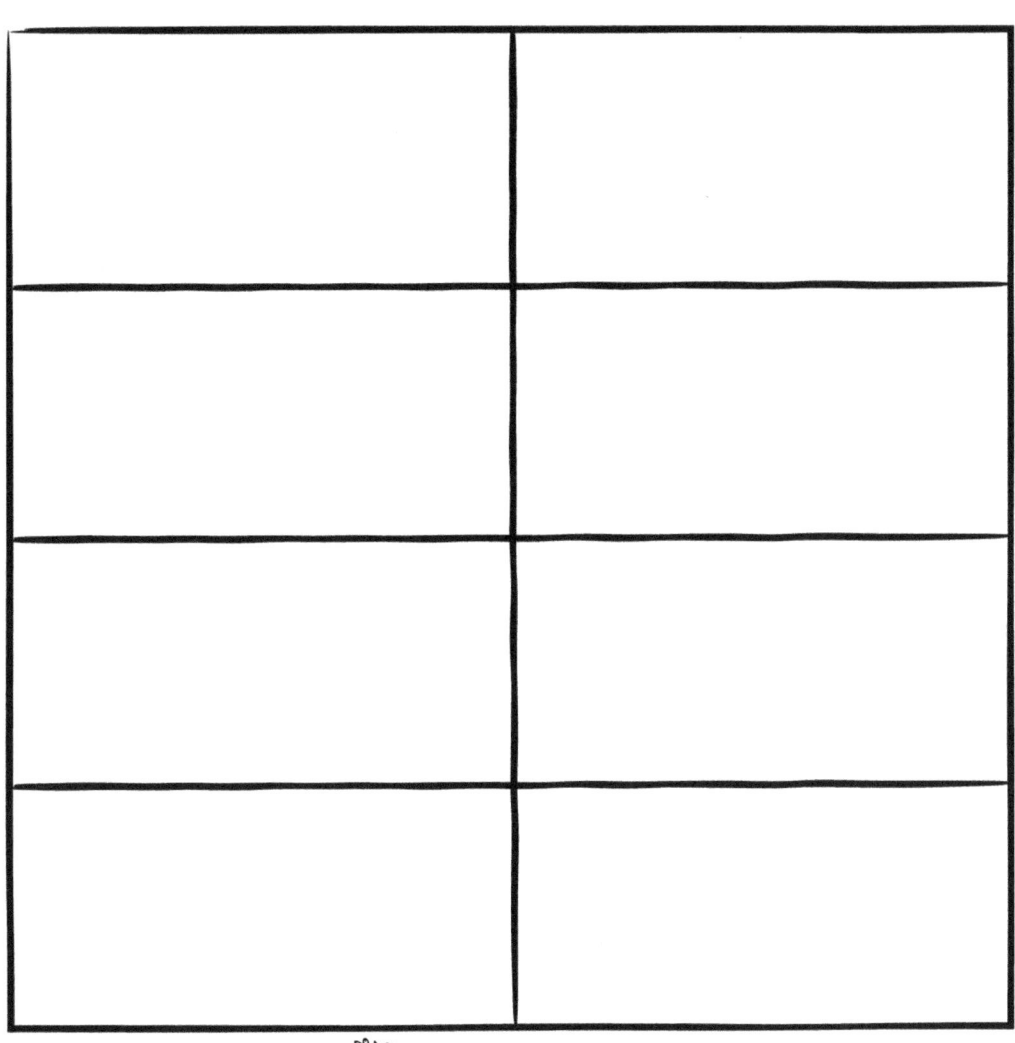

The Gift of Enough

Self-care is more than candle scented air.

More than hands that tame her hair.

It's quiet moments, deep and true.

A gentle grace she's owed, she's due.

It's knowing when her heart is sore,

When less is needed, never more.

It's holding space, it's saying no,

Without the weight of guilt in tow.

To rest, to breathe, to simply be,

Without a goal, a need, a plea.

For she is worthy, whole, and free—

Not just in giving, but in being she.

Self Discovery

THE POEM SUGGESTS SELF-CARE GOES BEYOND PAMPERING. WHAT DOES 'ENOUGH' LOOK LIKE FOR YOU IN TERMS OF CARING FOR YOUR WELL-BEING?

_____

_____

_____

_____

_____

HOW DO SETTING BOUNDARIES AND SAYING 'NO' WITHOUT GUILT CONTRIBUTE TO YOUR OVERALL WELL-BEING AND SENSE OF SELF-WORTH?

_____

_____

_____

_____

_____

Self Discovery

---·❖—❖·---

"IT'S HOLDING SPACE. IT'S SAYING NO, WITHOUT THE WEIGHT OF GUILT IN TOW." CAN YOU SET
BOUNDARIES AND SAY NO? DESCRIBE THE SCENARIO:

_____

_____

_____

_____

_____

_____

IN THE ABOVE SCENARIO, DID YOU FEEL GUILTY OR FEEL THE NEED TO JUSTIFY OR MAKE IT UP SOMEHOW? EXPLAIN
WHY AND WHAT YOU DID TO ALLEVIATE THE FEELING. DO YOU FEEL IT WAS A HEALTHY BALANCE?

_____

_____

_____

_____

_____

_____

Self Discovery

RE-READ THE POEM. IN THE BOXES ON THE LEFT SIDE-LIST 4 EXPRESSIONS OF SELF-CARE YOU WANT TO INCORPORATE IN YOUR LIFE'S ROUTINES. EXPLAIN WHY AND HOW OFTEN YOU WANT TO EXPERIENCE IT. ON THE RIGHT SIDE OF EACH LIST WHAT STEPS OR HOW ARE YOU GOING TO ADD AND MAINTAIN THIS REGIME:

Journal Page

THIS IS YOUR SPACE TO REFLECT. ASK YOUR OWN QUESTIONS.. HERE ARE A FEW TO GET YOUR SELF-EXPLORATION STARTED:

- WHAT SURPRISED ME THE MOST ABOUT MY ANSWERS?

- WHICH POEM OR QUESTION WAS THE HARDEST TO ANSWER AND WHY?

- WHAT RESONATED WITH ME THE MOST?

- WHAT DO I THINK WILL CHANGE THE MOST WHEN I COME BACK FOR THE NEXT SECTION?

REMEMBER THERE IS NO RIGHT OR WRONG ANSWER. THIS IS ABOUT GROWTH AND SELF-REFLECTION

Section Three

REMEMBER TO COMPLETE THIS SECTION FULLY BEFORE MOVING ON. AND DON'T FORGET TO PAPERCLIP 📎 WHEN YOU'RE DONE!.

Rising from the Deep

SHE SWAM THROUGH WATERS, DARK AND DEEP,

WHERE SHADOWS CURLED AND SILENCE WEEPED.

YET WITH EACH STROKE, HER SPIRIT GREW,

FOR DARKNESS FORGED WHAT LIGHT ONCE KNEW.

EMERGING, BREATHLESS, ON THE SHORE,

SHE FELT THE WEIGHT OF FEAR NO MORE.

THE NIGHT HAD SHAPED HER, FIERCE AND FREE——

A STRENGTH SHE NEVER THOUGHT COULD BE.

Self Discovery

---◆◦◆━━◆◦◆---

WHAT FEELING OR IMAGE DOES THIS POEM EVOKE ABOUT YOU?

_____

_____

_____

_____

_____

_____

WHAT STRENGTH OR RESILIENCE DO YOU SEE REFLECTED IN THE POEM?

_____

_____

_____

_____

_____

_____

_____

Self Discovery

HOW CAN YOU APPLY THE MESSAGE OF THIS POEM TO YOUR OWN LIFE?

_____

_____

_____

_____

_____

_____

WHAT DOES THE PHRASE "DARKNESS FORGED WHAT LIGHT ONCE KNEW" MEAN TO YOU?

_____

_____

_____

_____

_____

_____

Self Discovery

RE-READ THE POEM, AND DRAW THE FIRST THING THAT COMES TO MIND:

(It's not about how well you draw, it's about self reflection. Use words and symbols if it helps. This is about you and your feelings.)

One with the Infinite

SHE GAZED UPON THE ENDLESS SKY,

A SEA OF STARS SO VAST, SO HIGH.

FOR A MOMENT, SHE FELT SO SMALL,

A FLEETING SPARK, A WHISPERED CALL.

BUT THEN THE NIGHT BREATHED SOFT AND TRUE,

ITS QUIET PULSE, A GENTLE CLUE——

SHE WAS NOT ALONE, NOT SET APART,

BUT WOVEN DEEP WITHIN ITS HEART.

THE COSMOS HUMMED, THE HEAVENS SWAYED,

AND IN THEIR DANCE, HER SOUL OBEYED.

NOT LOST, NOT LESS, NOT CAST ASIDE——

BUT PART OF ALL, THE ENDLESS TIDE.

Self Discovery

—◆◆—◆◆—

WHAT FEELING OR IMAGE DOES THIS POEM EVOKE ABOUT YOU?

_____

_____

_____

_____

_____

_____

HOW DOES THIS POEM MAKE YOU FEEL ABOUT YOUR PLACE IN THE UNIVERSE?

_____

_____

_____

_____

_____

_____

Self Discovery

WHAT DOES THE LINE "PART OF ALL, THE ENDLESS TIDE" MEAN TO YOU?

_____

_____

_____

_____

_____

_____

HOW DOES FEELING LONELY DIFFER FROM BEING ALONE, AND HOW DOES THIS AFFECT YOU?

_____

_____

_____

_____

_____

_____

Self Discovery

---◆◇◆◇---

RE-READ THE POEM, AND DRAW YOURSELF IN THE UNIVERSE::

(It's not about how well you draw, it's about self reflection. Use words
and symbols if it helps. This is about you and your feelings.)

The Beauty in Difference

WE STAND AS SISTERS. SIDE BY SIDE.

THE SAME IN HEART. IN LOVE. IN PRIDE.

YET IN OUR THREADS OF GOLD AND LIGHT.

NO TWO ARE WOVEN QUITE ALIKE.

YOUR FIRE BURNS. MY RIVER FLOWS.

YOUR PETALS BLOOM. MY WILD WIND BLOWS.

AND IN THE SPACES WHERE WE PART.

LIES THE BRILLIANCE OF OUR ART.

NOT MEANT TO BLEND. NOR FADE AWAY.

BUT SHINE IN OUR OWN FEARLESS WAY.

FOR EVERY VOICE. FOR EVERY HUE.

THE WORLD IS BRIGHTER——WITH ME AND YOU.

Self Discovery

WRITE WHAT THIS POEM MEANS TO YOU, AND APPLY IT TO ONE ASPECT OF YOUR LIFE:

_____

_____

_____

_____

_____

_____

_____

WHAT 'FIRE BURNS' OR 'RIVER FLOWS' WITHIN YOU? WHAT MAKES YOUR SPIRIT UNIQUELY VIBRANT?

_____

_____

_____

_____

_____

_____

_____

Self Discovery

WHAT DOES THE LINE "AND IN THE SPACES WHERE WE PART, LIES THE BRILLIANCE OF OUR ART." MEAN TO YOU?

_____

_____

_____

_____

_____

_____

DO YOU FEEL LIKE FITTING IN MEANS TO EMULATE OTHERS OR DO YOU TRY TO FIND SOMETHING SIMILAR BUT DIFFERENT WITHIN YOURSELF?

_____

_____

_____

_____

_____

_____

Self Discovery

RE-READ THE POEM. AND WRITE DOWN A STRENGTH IN EACH BOX AND 3-5 THINGS YOU CAN/COULD ACCOMPLISH WITH IT (EVEN IF YOU HAVEN'T YET)::

(It's not about how well you draw, it's about self reflection. Use words and symbols if it helps. This is about you and your feelings.)

Dare to Begin

SHE STANDS BEFORE THE TOWERING CLIMB.

A DREAM SO VAST. A TEST OF TIME.

DOUBT LINGERS CLOSE. A VOICE SO SLIGHT——

WHAT IF I'M WRONG? WHAT IF I'M RIGHT?

BUT MOUNTAINS RISE THROUGH WIND AND STONE.

AND SEEDS BREAK EARTH TO STAND ALONE.

NO JOURNEY STARTS WITH CERTAIN GROUND.

BUT WITH THE COURAGE TO BE FOUND.

SO LET HER STUMBLE. LET HER BEND.

EACH FALL A STEP. NOT JOURNEY'S END.

FOR IN THE CRACKS. THE LIGHT SHINES THROUGH——

PROOF SHE IS STRONG. AND GROWING TOO.

SHE TAKES A BREATH. SHE DARES TO TRY——

FOR EVEN WINGS MUST FAIL TO FLY.

Self Discovery

WHAT 'TOWERING CLIMB' OR DREAM IS CALLING TO YOU? WHAT IS THE FIRST STEP YOU NEED TO TAKE TO BEGIN?

_____

_____

_____

_____

_____

_____

WHAT 'VOICE OF DOUBT' IS WHISPERING IN YOUR EAR? HOW CAN YOU FIND THE COURAGE TO QUIET IT AND 'DARE TO BEGIN'?

_____

_____

_____

_____

_____

_____

Self Discovery

THINK ABOUT SOMETHING YOU ACCOMPLISHED, WHICH HAD A FAILED ATTEMPT, AND DESCRIBE WHAT YOU CHANGED TO TURN IT AROUND AND SUCCEED:

_____

_____

_____

_____

_____

_____

HOW DOES THE IDEA THAT "EACH FALL A STEP, NOT JOURNEY'S END" RESONATE WITH YOU?

_____

_____

_____

_____

_____

_____

Self Discovery

RE-READ THE POEM, AND WRITE A 4 STEP PLAN ON HOW YOU CAN CONQUER THE MOUNTAIN -WRITE DETAILS FOR EACH STEP INCLUDE ANY FORESEEABLE PITFALLS. YOU NEED TO HAVE AT LEAST ONE POSSIBLE WAY AROUND IT:

(It's not about how well you draw, it's about self reflection. Use words and symbols if it helps. This is about you and your feelings.)

Found Within

SHE SEARCHED THE WORLD, BOTH FAR AND WIDE,

THROUGH FLEETING JOYS AND CHANGING TIDES,

IN EVERY FACE, IN EVERY PLACE,

SHE CHASED A LIGHT SHE COULD NOT SEE AND COULD NOT TRACE.

SHE REACHED BEYOND, HER HEART UNSURE,

FOR SOMETHING DISTANT, SOMETHING PURE,

YET ALL SHE SOUGHT HAD ALWAYS BEEN——

A QUIET FLAME THAT BURNED WITHIN.

NOT IN ANOTHER, NOT IN THE VIEW,

BUT IN HER OWN HEART, STRONG AND TRUE,

HAPPINESS WHISPERED, SOFT YET CLEAR——

YOU WERE NEVER LOST, I WAS ALWAYS HERE.

Self Discovery

THE POEM DESCRIBES SEARCHING 'THE WORLD, BOTH FAR AND WIDE.' WHERE HAVE YOU LOOKED FOR HAPPINESS OR FULFILLMENT IN YOUR LIFE?

_____

_____

_____

_____

_____

_____

WHAT EXTERNAL THINGS DO YOU SOMETIMES RELY ON FOR HAPPINESS OR VALIDATION? IS IT PEOPLE? FOOD? SHOPPING?

_____

_____

_____

_____

_____

_____

Self Discovery

CAN YOU IDENTIFY WITH THE FEELING OF SEARCHING FOR SOMETHING "DISTANT, SOMETHING PURE"?

WHAT DO YOU THINK THAT "SOMETHING" REPRESENTS FOR YOU?

_____

_____

_____

_____

_____

_____

NAME A TIME WHEN YOU HAVE FELT THAT "QUIET FLAME" OF HAPPINESS BURN WITHIN. WHAT SPARKED IT?

_____

_____

_____

_____

_____

_____

Self Discovery

RE-READ THE POEM. NOW, IMAGINE YOUR FLAME AND DRAW IT. USE COLORS THAT REPRESENT THE HAPPINESS AND THE GLOW YOU SEE. FEEL FREE TO ADD THINGS WITHIN YOU THAT FEED THE FLAME:

(It's not about how well you draw, it's about self reflection. Use words and symbols if it helps. This is about you and your feelings.)

Words we Weave

She laughed it off. a casual phrase.

A joke she thought would fade like haze.

Yet words take root. they start to bloom.

And what you speak, your soul consumes.

.

A fleeting slight, a thoughtless jest,

Can carve a doubt within the breast,

Her mind won't question if it's true——

It holds each word and shapes anew.

So let her speak with kindness' art,

To lift herself, to heal, to start,

For every thought, each word she sows,

Becomes the path on which she goes.

Self Discovery

———————◆◆◆———————

WHAT DOES THE LINE "YET WORDS TAKE ROOT. THEY START TO BLOOM. AND WHAT YOU SPEAK. YOUR SOUL CONSUMES" MEAN TO YOU?.

_____

_____

_____

_____

_____

_____

HOW MIGHT BEING MINDFUL OF 'A FLEETING SLIGHT. A THOUGHTLESS JEST.' CHANGE HOW YOU SPEAK TO AND ABOUT YOURSELF?

_____

_____

_____

_____

_____

_____

Self Discovery

HOW DOES THE IDEA THAT "EVERY THOUGHT, EACH WORD SHE SOWS, BECOMES THE PATH ON WHICH SHE GOES" RESONATE WITH YOU?

_____

_____

_____

_____

_____

_____

RE-READ THE POEM—DOES THE MESSAGE SEEM SILLY OR DOESN'T APPLY TO YOU? IT SO, WHY?

_____

_____

_____

_____

_____

_____

Self Discovery

RE-READ THE POEM. COLLECT 4 THINGS YOU HAVE SAID ABOUT OR TO YOURSELF RECENTLY. PUT THOSE IN THE BOXES ON THE LEFT SIDE. ON THE RIGHT SIDE. WRITE WHAT WOULD YOU HAVE SAID TO A CLOSE FRIEND UNDER SIMILAR CIRCUMSTANCES:

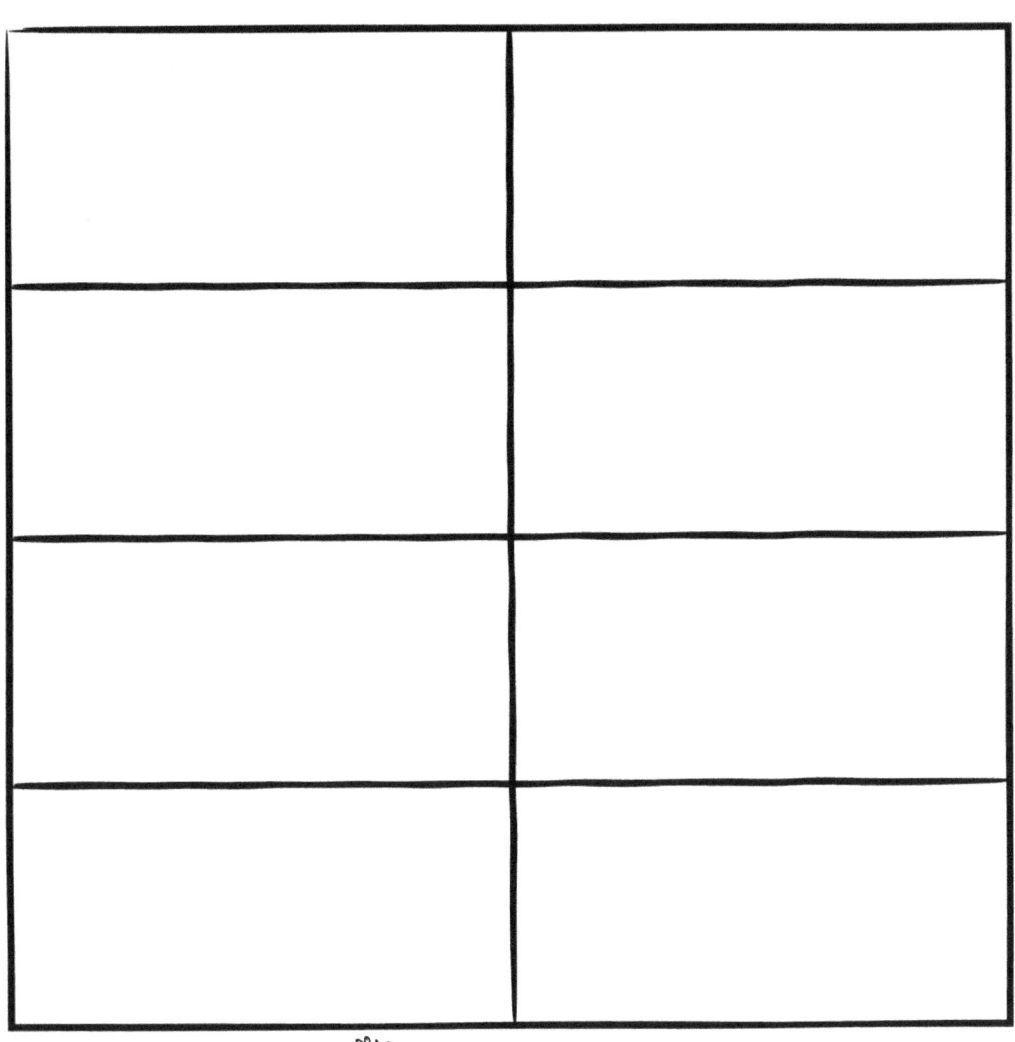

The Gift of Enough

SELF-CARE IS MORE THAN CANDLE SCENTED AIR,

MORE THAN HANDS THAT TAME HER HAIR.

IT'S QUIET MOMENTS, DEEP AND TRUE,

A GENTLE GRACE SHE'S OWED, SHE'S DUE.

IT'S KNOWING WHEN HER HEART IS SORE,

WHEN LESS IS NEEDED, NEVER MORE.

IT'S HOLDING SPACE, IT'S SAYING NO,

WITHOUT THE WEIGHT OF GUILT IN TOW.

TO REST, TO BREATHE, TO SIMPLY BE,

WITHOUT A GOAL, A NEED, A PLEA.

FOR SHE IS WORTHY, WHOLE, AND FREE——

NOT JUST IN GIVING, BUT IN BEING SHE.

Self Discovery

THE POEM SUGGESTS SELF-CARE GOES BEYOND PAMPERING. WHAT DOES 'ENOUGH' LOOK LIKE FOR YOU IN TERMS OF CARING FOR YOUR WELL-BEING?

_____

_____

_____

_____

_____

_____

HOW DO SETTING BOUNDARIES AND SAYING 'NO' WITHOUT GUILT CONTRIBUTE TO YOUR OVERALL WELL-BEING AND SENSE OF SELF-WORTH?

_____

_____

_____

_____

_____

_____

Self Discovery

"IT'S HOLDING SPACE, IT'S SAYING NO, WITHOUT THE WEIGHT OF GUILT IN TOW." CAN YOU SET BOUNDARIES AND SAY NO? DESCRIBE THE SCENARIO:

_____

_____

_____

_____

_____

_____

_____

IN THE ABOVE SCENARIO, DID YOU FEEL GUILTY OR FEEL THE NEED TO JUSTIFY OR MAKE IT UP SOMEHOW? EXPLAIN WHY AND WHAT YOU DID TO ALLEVIATE THE FEELING. DO YOU FEEL IT WAS A HEALTHY BALANCE?

_____

_____

_____

_____

_____

_____

Self Discovery

RE-READ THE POEM. IN THE BOXES ON THE LEFT SIDE-LIST 4 EXPRESSIONS OF SELF-CARE YOU WANT TO INCORPORATE IN YOUR LIFE'S ROUTINES. EXPLAIN WHY AND HOW OFTEN YOU WANT TO EXPERIENCE IT. ON THE RIGHT SIDE OF EACH LIST WHAT STEPS OR HOW ARE YOU GOING TO ADD AND MAINTAIN THIS REGIME:

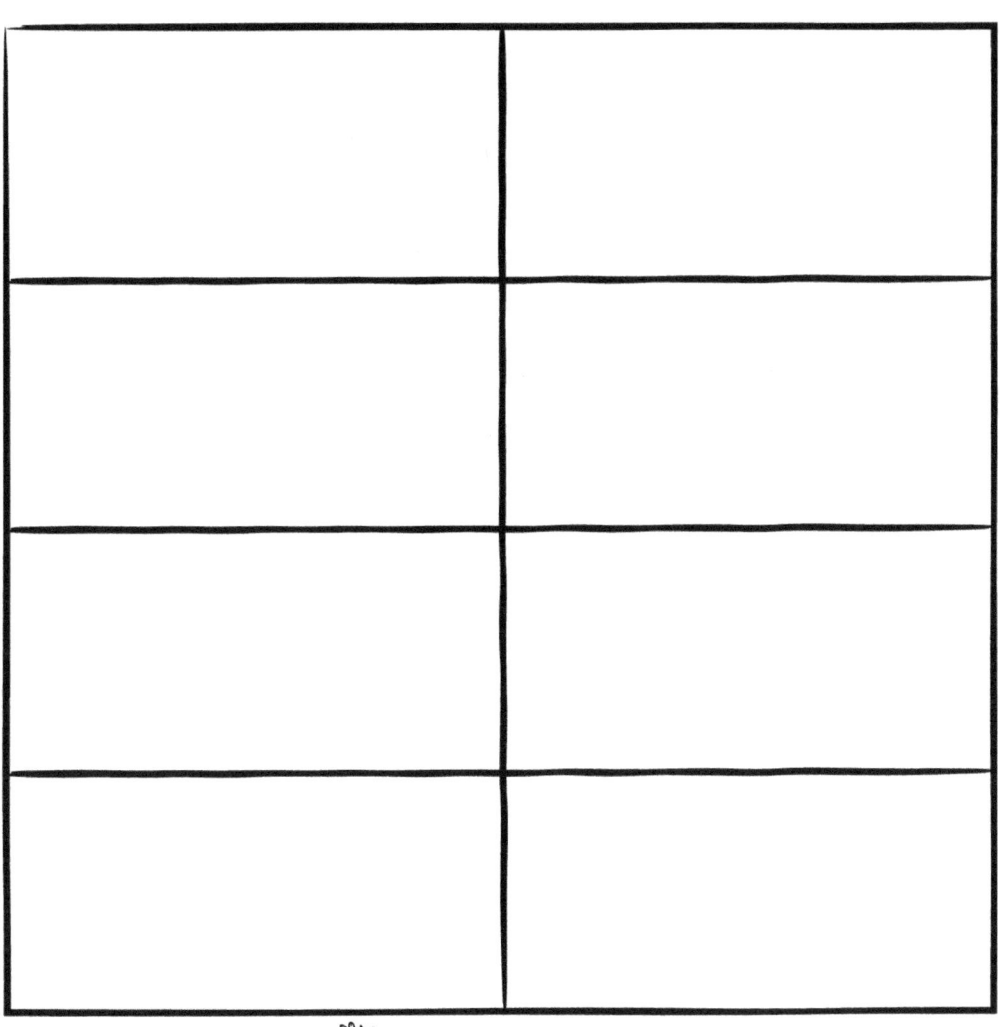

Journal Page

THIS IS YOUR SPACE TO REFLECT. ASK YOUR OWN QUESTIONS.. HERE ARE A FEW TO GET YOUR SELF-EXPLORATION STARTED:

- WHAT SURPRISED ME THE MOST ABOUT MY ANSWERS?

- WHICH POEM OR QUESTION WAS THE HARDEST TO ANSWER AND WHY?

- WHAT RESONATED WITH ME THE MOST?

- WHAT DO I THINK WILL CHANGE THE MOST WHEN I COME BACK FOR THE NEXT SECTION?

REMEMBER THERE IS NO RIGHT OR WRONG ANSWER. THIS IS ABOUT GROWTH AND SELF-REFLECTION

_____

_____

_____

_____

_____

_____

_____

_____

_____

_____

_____

_____

_____

Section Four

REMEMBER TO COMPLETE THIS SECTION FULLY BEFORE MOVING ON. AND DON'T FORGET TO PAPERCLIP 📎 WHEN YOU'RE DONE!.

Rising from the Deep

SHE SWAM THROUGH WATERS, DARK AND DEEP,

WHERE SHADOWS CURLED AND SILENCE WEEPED.

YET WITH EACH STROKE, HER SPIRIT GREW,

FOR DARKNESS FORGED WHAT LIGHT ONCE KNEW.

EMERGING, BREATHLESS, ON THE SHORE,

SHE FELT THE WEIGHT OF FEAR NO MORE.

THE NIGHT HAD SHAPED HER, FIERCE AND FREE——

A STRENGTH SHE NEVER THOUGHT COULD BE.

Self Discovery

WHAT FEELING OR IMAGE DOES THIS POEM EVOKE ABOUT YOU?

_____

_____

_____

_____

_____

_____

WHAT STRENGTH OR RESILIENCE DO YOU SEE REFLECTED IN THE POEM?

_____

_____

_____

_____

_____

_____

Self Discovery

HOW CAN YOU APPLY THE MESSAGE OF THIS POEM TO YOUR OWN LIFE?

_____

_____

_____

_____

_____

_____

_____

WHAT DOES THE PHRASE "DARKNESS FORGED WHAT LIGHT ONCE KNEW" MEAN TO YOU?

_____

_____

_____

_____

_____

_____

_____

Self Discovery

RE-READ THE POEM, AND DRAW THE FIRST THING THAT COMES TO MIND:

(It's not about how well you draw, it's about self reflection. Use words and symbols if it helps. This is about you and your feelings.)

One with the Infinite

SHE GAZED UPON THE ENDLESS SKY.

A SEA OF STARS SO VAST. SO HIGH.

FOR A MOMENT. SHE FELT SO SMALL.

A FLEETING SPARK. A WHISPERED CALL.

BUT THEN THE NIGHT BREATHED SOFT AND TRUE.

ITS QUIET PULSE. A GENTLE CLUE——

SHE WAS NOT ALONE. NOT SET APART.

BUT WOVEN DEEP WITHIN ITS HEART.

THE COSMOS HUMMED. THE HEAVENS SWAYED.

AND IN THEIR DANCE. HER SOUL OBEYED.

NOT LOST. NOT LESS. NOT CAST ASIDE——

BUT PART OF ALL. THE ENDLESS TIDE.

Self Discovery

WHAT FEELING OR IMAGE DOES THIS POEM EVOKE ABOUT YOU?

_____

_____

_____

_____

_____

_____

HOW DOES THIS POEM MAKE YOU FEEL ABOUT YOUR PLACE IN THE UNIVERSE?

_____

_____

_____

_____

_____

_____

Self Discovery

WHAT DOES THE LINE "PART OF ALL, THE ENDLESS TIDE" MEAN TO YOU?

_____

_____

_____

_____

_____

_____

HOW DOES FEELING LONELY DIFFER FROM BEING ALONE, AND HOW DOES THIS AFFECT YOU?

_____

_____

_____

_____

_____

Self Discovery

RE-READ THE POEM, AND DRAW YOURSELF IN THE UNIVERSE::

(It's not about how well you draw, it's about self reflection. Use words and symbols if it helps. This is about you and your feelings.)

The Beauty in Difference

WE STAND AS SISTERS. SIDE BY SIDE.

THE SAME IN HEART. IN LOVE. IN PRIDE.

YET IN OUR THREADS OF GOLD AND LIGHT,

NO TWO ARE WOVEN QUITE ALIKE.

YOUR FIRE BURNS. MY RIVER FLOWS,

YOUR PETALS BLOOM. MY WILD WIND BLOWS,

AND IN THE SPACES WHERE WE PART,

LIES THE BRILLIANCE OF OUR ART.

NOT MEANT TO BLEND. NOR FADE AWAY,

BUT SHINE IN OUR OWN FEARLESS WAY.

FOR EVERY VOICE. FOR EVERY HUE,

THE WORLD IS BRIGHTER——WITH ME AND YOU.

Self Discovery

---❧◆❧◆❧---

WRITE WHAT THIS POEM MEANS TO YOU, AND APPLY IT TO ONE ASPECT OF YOUR LIFE:

_____

_____

_____

_____

_____

_____

_____

WHAT 'FIRE BURNS' OR 'RIVER FLOWS' WITHIN YOU? WHAT MAKES YOUR SPIRIT UNIQUELY VIBRANT?

_____

_____

_____

_____

_____

_____

Self Discovery

---◆❧◆❧◆---

WHAT DOES THE LINE "AND IN THE SPACES WHERE WE PART, LIES THE BRILLIANCE OF OUR ART." MEAN TO YOU?

_____

_____

_____

_____

_____

_____

DO YOU FEEL LIKE FITTING IN MEANS TO EMULATE OTHERS OR DO YOU TRY TO FIND SOMETHING SIMILAR BUT DIFFERENT WITHIN YOURSELF?

_____

_____

_____

_____

_____

_____

Self Discovery

RE-READ THE POEM, AND WRITE DOWN A STRENGTH IN EACH BOX AND 3-5 THINGS YOU CAN/COULD ACCOMPLISH WITH IT (EVEN IF YOU HAVEN'T YET):.

(It's not about how well you draw, it's about self reflection. Use words and symbols if it helps. This is about you and your feelings.)

Dare to Begin

She stands before the towering climb.
A dream so vast. A test of time.
Doubt lingers close. A voice so slight—
What if I'm wrong? What if I'm right?

But mountains rise through wind and stone.
And seeds break earth to stand alone.
No journey starts with certain ground.
But with the courage to be found.

So let her stumble. Let her bend.
Each fall a step. Not journey's end.
For in the cracks. the light shines through—
Proof she is strong. and growing too.

She takes a breath. she dares to try—
For even wings must fail to fly.

Self Discovery

WHAT 'TOWERING CLIMB' OR DREAM IS CALLING TO YOU? WHAT IS THE FIRST STEP YOU NEED TO TAKE TO BEGIN?

_____

_____

_____

_____

_____

_____

WHAT 'VOICE OF DOUBT' IS WHISPERING IN YOUR EAR? HOW CAN YOU FIND THE COURAGE TO QUIET IT AND

'DARE TO BEGIN'?

_____

_____

_____

_____

_____

_____

Self Discovery

THINK ABOUT SOMETHING YOU ACCOMPLISHED, WHICH HAD A FAILED ATTEMPT, AND DESCRIBE WHAT YOU CHANGED TO TURN IT AROUND AND SUCCEED:

_____

_____

_____

_____

_____

_____

HOW DOES THE IDEA THAT "EACH FALL A STEP, NOT JOURNEY'S END" RESONATE WITH YOU?

_____

_____

_____

_____

_____

Self Discovery

RE-READ THE POEM, AND WRITE A 4 STEP PLAN ON HOW YOU CAN CONQUER THE MOUNTAIN -WRITE DETAILS FOR EACH STEP INCLUDE ANY FORESEEABLE PITFALLS. YOU NEED TO HAVE AT LEAST ONE POSSIBLE WAY AROUND IT:

(It's not about how well you draw, it's about self reflection. Use words and symbols if it helps. This is about you and your feelings.)

Found Within

SHE SEARCHED THE WORLD, BOTH FAR AND WIDE,

THROUGH FLEETING JOYS AND CHANGING TIDES.

IN EVERY FACE, IN EVERY PLACE,

SHE CHASED A LIGHT SHE COULD NOT SEE AND COULD NOT TRACE.

SHE REACHED BEYOND, HER HEART UNSURE,

FOR SOMETHING DISTANT, SOMETHING PURE,

YET ALL SHE SOUGHT HAD ALWAYS BEEN——

A QUIET FLAME THAT BURNED WITHIN.

NOT IN ANOTHER, NOT IN THE VIEW,

BUT IN HER OWN HEART, STRONG AND TRUE,

HAPPINESS WHISPERED, SOFT YET CLEAR——

YOU WERE NEVER LOST, I WAS ALWAYS HERE.

Self Discovery

THE POEM DESCRIBES SEARCHING 'THE WORLD, BOTH FAR AND WIDE.' WHERE HAVE YOU LOOKED FOR HAPPINESS OR FULFILLMENT IN YOUR LIFE?

_____

_____

_____

_____

_____

_____

_____

WHAT EXTERNAL THINGS DO YOU SOMETIMES RELY ON FOR HAPPINESS OR VALIDATION? IS IT PEOPLE? FOOD? SHOPPING?

_____

_____

_____

_____

_____

_____

Self Discovery

CAN YOU IDENTIFY WITH THE FEELING OF SEARCHING FOR SOMETHING "DISTANT, SOMETHING PURE"?
WHAT DO YOU THINK THAT "SOMETHING" REPRESENTS FOR YOU?

_____

_____

_____

_____

_____

_____

NAME A TIME WHEN YOU HAVE FELT THAT "QUIET FLAME" OF HAPPINESS BURN WITHIN. WHAT SPARKED IT?

_____

_____

_____

_____

_____

_____

Self Discovery

RE-READ THE POEM. NOW, IMAGINE YOUR FLAME AND DRAW IT. USE COLORS THAT REPRESENT THE HAPPINESS AND THE GLOW YOU SEE. FEEL FREE TO ADD THINGS WITHIN YOU THAT FEED THE FLAME:

(It's not about how well you draw, it's about self reflection. Use words and symbols if it helps. This is about you and your feelings.)

Words we Weave

SHE LAUGHED IT OFF. A CASUAL PHRASE.

A JOKE SHE THOUGHT WOULD FADE LIKE HAZE.

YET WORDS TAKE ROOT. THEY START TO BLOOM,

AND WHAT YOU SPEAK. YOUR SOUL CONSUMES.

.

A FLEETING SLIGHT. A THOUGHTLESS JEST.

CAN CARVE A DOUBT WITHIN THE BREAST.

HER MIND WON'T QUESTION IF IT'S TRUE —

IT HOLDS EACH WORD AND SHAPES ANEW.

SO LET HER SPEAK WITH KINDNESS' ART.

TO LIFT HERSELF. TO HEAL. TO START.

FOR EVERY THOUGHT. EACH WORD SHE SOWS.

BECOMES THE PATH ON WHICH SHE GOES.

Self Discovery

WHAT DOES THE LINE "YET WORDS TAKE ROOT, THEY START TO BLOOM, AND WHAT YOU SPEAK, YOUR SOUL CONSUMES" MEAN TO YOU?.

_____

_____

_____

_____

_____

_____

HOW MIGHT BEING MINDFUL OF 'A FLEETING SLIGHT, A THOUGHTLESS JEST,' CHANGE HOW YOU SPEAK TO AND ABOUT YOURSELF?

_____

_____

_____

_____

_____

_____

Self Discovery

HOW DOES THE IDEA THAT "EVERY THOUGHT, EACH WORD SHE SOWS, BECOMES THE PATH ON WHICH SHE GOES" RESONATE WITH YOU?

_____

_____

_____

_____

_____

_____

RE-READ THE POEM—DOES THE MESSAGE SEEM SILLY OR DOESN'T APPLY TO YOU? IT SO, WHY?

_____

_____

_____

_____

_____

Self Discovery

RE-READ THE POEM. COLLECT 4 THINGS YOU HAVE SAID ABOUT OR TO YOURSELF RECENTLY. PUT THOSE IN THE BOXES ON THE LEFT SIDE. ON THE RIGHT SIDE, WRITE WHAT WOULD YOU HAVE SAID TO A CLOSE FRIEND UNDER SIMILAR CIRCUMSTANCES:

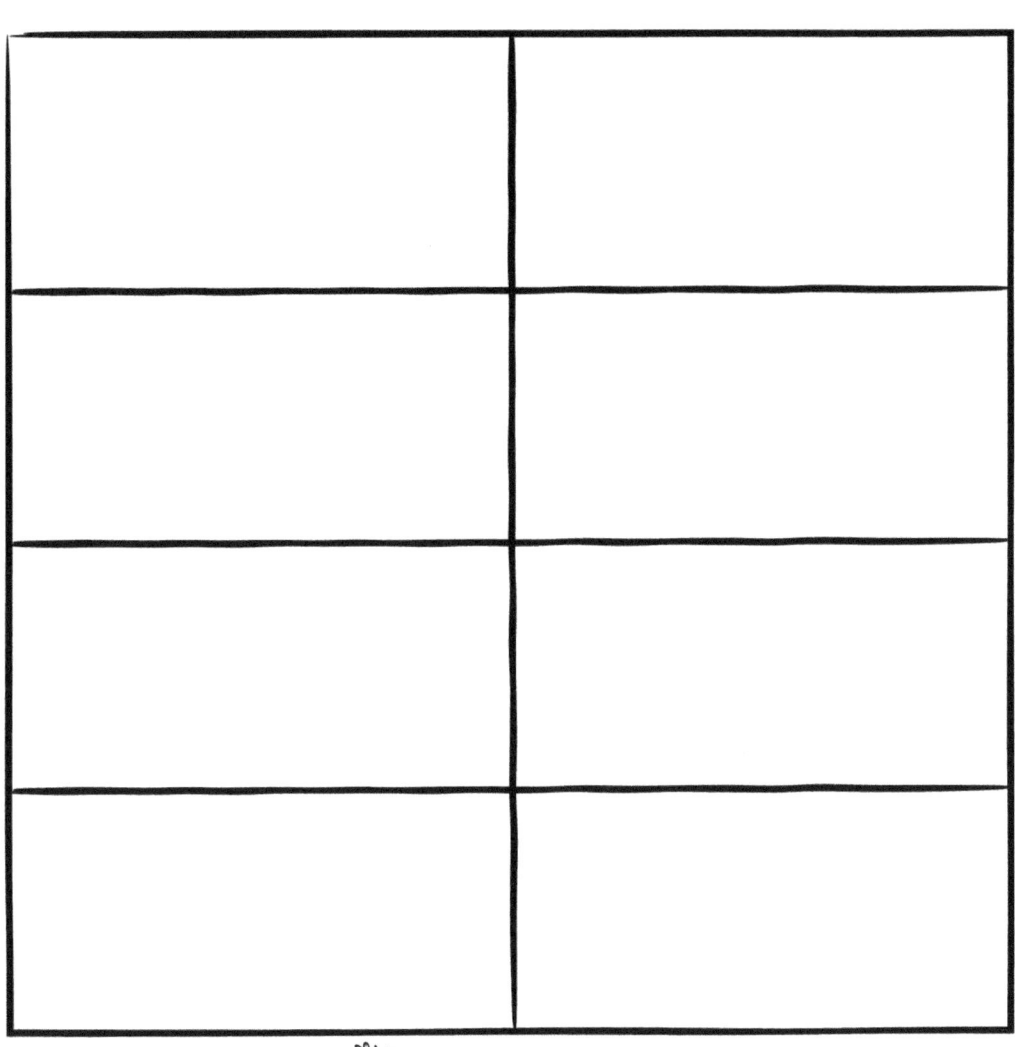

The Gift of Enough

SELF-CARE IS MORE THAN CANDLE SCENTED AIR,

MORE THAN HANDS THAT TAME HER HAIR.

IT'S QUIET MOMENTS, DEEP AND TRUE,

A GENTLE GRACE SHE'S OWED, SHE'S DUE.

IT'S KNOWING WHEN HER HEART IS SORE,

WHEN LESS IS NEEDED, NEVER MORE.

IT'S HOLDING SPACE, IT'S SAYING NO,

WITHOUT THE WEIGHT OF GUILT IN TOW.

TO REST, TO BREATHE, TO SIMPLY BE,

WITHOUT A GOAL, A NEED, A PLEA.

FOR SHE IS WORTHY, WHOLE, AND FREE—

NOT JUST IN GIVING, BUT IN BEING SHE.

Self Discovery

THE POEM SUGGESTS SELF-CARE GOES BEYOND PAMPERING. WHAT DOES 'ENOUGH' LOOK LIKE FOR YOU IN TERMS OF CARING FOR YOUR WELL-BEING?

_____

_____

_____

_____

_____

_____

HOW DO SETTING BOUNDARIES AND SAYING 'NO' WITHOUT GUILT CONTRIBUTE TO YOUR OVERALL WELL-BEING AND SENSE OF SELF-WORTH?

_____

_____

_____

_____

_____

_____

Self Discovery

"IT'S HOLDING SPACE, IT'S SAYING NO, WITHOUT THE WEIGHT OF GUILT IN TOW." CAN YOU SET BOUNDARIES AND SAY NO? DESCRIBE THE SCENARIO:

_____

_____

_____

_____

_____

_____

IN THE ABOVE SCENARIO, DID YOU FEEL GUILTY OR FEEL THE NEED TO JUSTIFY OR MAKE IT UP SOMEHOW? EXPLAIN WHY AND WHAT YOU DID TO ALLEVIATE THE FEELING. DO YOU FEEL IT WAS A HEALTHY BALANCE?

_____

_____

_____

_____

_____

_____

Self Discovery

RE-READ THE POEM. IN THE BOXES ON THE LEFT SIDE-LIST 4 EXPRESSIONS OF SELF-CARE YOU WANT TO INCORPORATE IN YOUR LIFE'S ROUTINES. EXPLAIN WHY AND HOW OFTEN YOU WANT TO EXPERIENCE IT. ON THE RIGHT SIDE OF EACH LIST WHAT STEPS OR HOW ARE YOU GOING TO ADD AND MAINTAIN THIS REGIME:

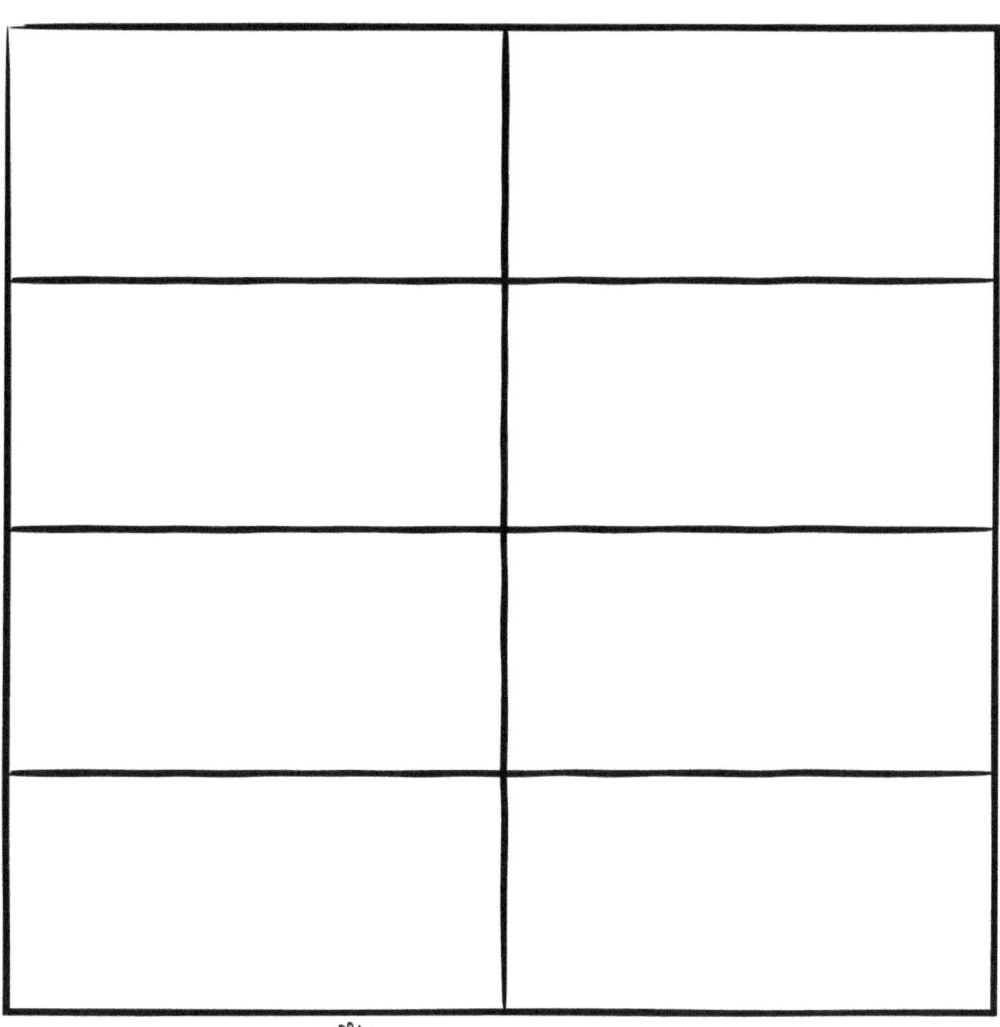

Journal Page

THIS IS YOUR SPACE TO REFLECT. ASK YOUR OWN QUESTIONS.. HERE ARE A FEW TO GET YOUR SELF-EXPLORATION STARTED:

- WHAT SURPRISED ME THE MOST ABOUT MY ANSWERS?

- WHICH POEM OR QUESTION WAS THE HARDEST TO ANSWER AND WHY?

- WHAT RESONATED WITH ME THE MOST?

- WHAT DO I THINK WILL CHANGE THE MOST WHEN I COME BACK FOR THE NEXT SECTION?

REMEMBER THERE IS NO RIGHT OR WRONG ANSWER. THIS IS ABOUT GROWTH AND SELF-REFLECTION

_____

_____

_____

_____

_____

_____

_____

_____

_____

_____

_____

_____

_____

_____

_____

www.ingramcontent.com/pod-product-compliance
Lightning Source LLC
Chambersburg PA
CBHW051851140626
46547CB00034BA/3084

* 9 7 9 8 2 1 8 6 2 1 9 9 5 *